My Identity as a Stereotypical Side Character
by
Marcus S. Campbell

Brick Cave Media
brickcavebooks.com

Brick Cave Media
brickcavebooks.com

A Note to You

Dear Reader,

I was so busy
trying to tame
your hectic heart
I had not realized
I had lost mine.
Along roads,
      and passageways,
          catacombs,
             and tombs of
the past is a piece of me
as part of a poem,
wrapped in a note,
addressed to you.

I love you even though we've never met.

Thank you,
Marcus

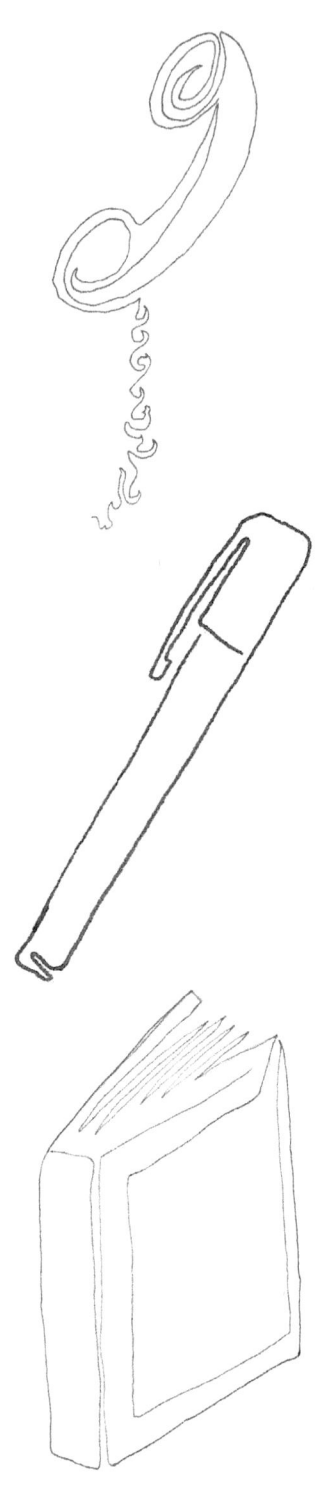

Table of Contents

Dedication:

This book is for all the people who stuck by my side through my years of trying to convince them to leave. It's dedicated to the people who propped me up instead of pulling me down. It's meant for all the people who helped shape me into who I am.

Lapsules are full of room to chill with less bills.

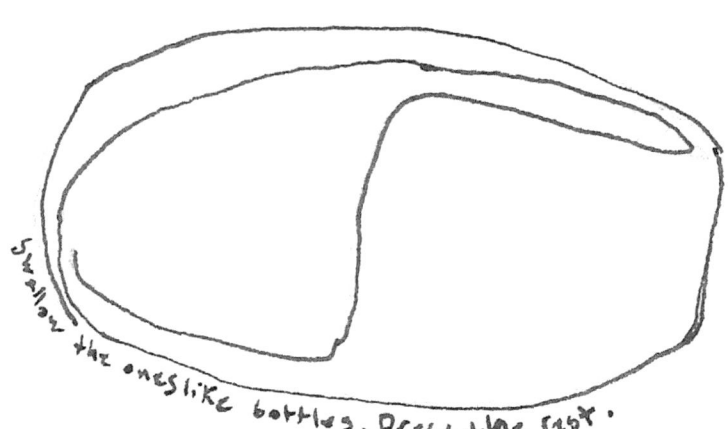

Swallow the ones like bottles. Press the rest.

Bars make fast cars go real slow

My Identity as a Stereotypical Side Character
by
Marcus Campbell

Brick Cave Media
brickcavebooks.com

My Identity as a Stereotypical Side Character

I'm a ghetto-blasting, ratchet, hood bastard
with a boom box shouldered like a bazooka
to tip Parental Advisories like rockets right toward Tipper Gore.
Tarzan, ignorant ape-man with a 40 in a brown bag,
a posted-up porch monkey waiting to cat call Mary Jane.
King Kong with a Magnum on, looking for white women.
The savage and the slave in your Lit. teachers' core curriculum,
the shadows and the jungle in the Heart of Darkness,
the Spear-Chucker Jones in this Mash-up.
A smooth Jazz cat with a conk
coming for your suburb, one 'rillo ride around your corner.
I am the probable cause, a right to detain,
armed with four wire wheels, rolling low and slow
a broken brake light leading to a pat down,
looking for 25-to-life tucked in my waist or taped to my taint.
The constant current of violence from sound bites of newscasts,
a threat strapped with a hoodie, ARIZONA tea,
and a knot of knotted hair.
The token Little Rascal who learned he wore his master's name
as he learned his place:
comic relief, thug, militant youth, hood-rat
like call-outs from children's toys:
a mouse's squeak, a pig's squeal, a mixed cow still saying moo

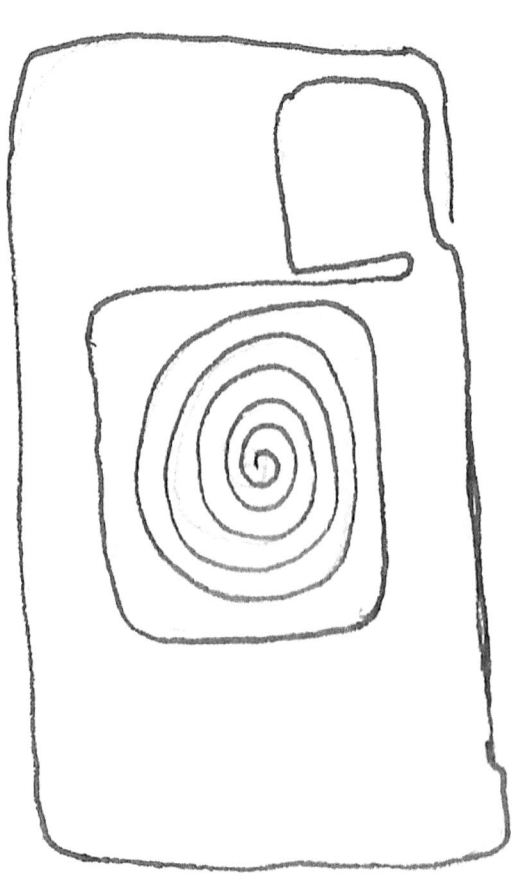

Micro Doses and Memory Boxes Don't Mix

I found a box old shit in the back corner of my closet,
in a cardboard box with the lid folded in on itself,
while on 50 microdots, third eye to God.

I jostled old trinkets around in the package,
pillaged memories and plundered
participation trophies and attendance medals,
gilded polyurethane vestiges to mediocrity.
Trophies for winning or losing
silly little pissing contests and games.

Like the one where you whipped each other
with a wound-up wet towel,
or the one where your friends
cornered you and sodomized you,
in the biblical sense,
while cackling with their books
in front of their belts.
Their adolescent excitement hidden
against hardcover calculus.

I would have preferred the game with the towels.
Those bruises would have stayed on the outside.
Boys play games I guess.

Like the one where they made me monkey
in the middle with my masculinity as bait.
Or rather than a ball, it'd be a flag
and they'd take turns capturing it.

I'm still stuck in jail, tying to win it back.
Some of us are still stuck in the locker room.

I pinched my eyes, till my brows kissed my cheeks,
attempted to will the trophies to ash,
scatter the dust in violent pitches across practice fields,
and gyms, and lecture rooms, hallways, and classes.

I wish I didn't have any trophies at all.
I rustled around relics and heard names that rang
like echoes of spells I wasn't supposed to cast
from grimoires I wasn't supposed to read.

Is scrolled past destinies in yearbooks
of people I shouldn't know:
my tormentor with a messiah complex
opened a furniture store in the desert
and married a whore;
the bushido bound green beret
killed himself in the service of nothing;
the girl who walked the path of Christ is dead.

I toss an old print out of my family crest, a boar
sworn to never forget,
along with a genealogy report
and citation for my accident,
or addiction, or failures,
together in a pale green folder.

I knew I wouldn't have enough space
to change lanes

but I did anyway and crashed
into the car in front of me.
I was disappointed when I woke up

to a pack of college kids clad in Luau garb,
gargling drunkenly and knocking on my window;
or maybe I'm in Hell, and everyone sees
happy-go-lucky, party-bound shamans when they die.

I barreled toward the bottom of the box
and practically punched my way through.
I had passed over all my treasure,
except the gold from when I sold my older soul.

I lingered for two seconds too long
over an old photo from senior prom
and was forced to remember
that unlike the other kids writhing on couches,
drunken, bare bodies to the universe
I couldn't seal the deal the night,

like so many sitcoms and movies assured me I would.
I couldn't seal the deal any night afterward.
I was an adult virgin.

The part that kept me searching
for the cold side of the pillow at 2 a.m.
wasn't that I was missing locker room talk,
I got plenty of that in between
the "hazing",
or that I haven't sowed those oats,

but that if sex is the physical manifestation of love
than nobody had ever said that they loved me.

Which was too say that I was unlovable,
empirically and provably un-loveable.

If I had kept a little black book, it would be empty,
as empty as the little spot in my wallet
that is perfect for a condom,
nestled right next to where I keep my joint papers
and last $11.

If every woman who said they loved me were a sea of gold,
I'd have cereal, tortillas, and dead ants in my pantry.
If all those lovely women were in that room,
I would still have been alone,

looking for junk in this box to pawn
to pay for my next session of E.M.D.R.
therapy while tip-toeing beyond the veil on L.S.D,
micro-dosing, whispering gently, taunted by Lucy
in Fur.

But I'm still here and I'm still me,
barreling toward the bottom of the box,
practically punching my way past,
tossed through all my treasure.
I snapped the box lid shut,
I'll keep what little I have left.

Crab Walk

"Your great-grandmother wrote crab poems"
Hawaiian beach, sun, smiles and
       in the ass crack type of poems.
       Forgot about the crack and meth
down the way type of poems.
That's just sand off the back
       of the crab whose mortgage loan is not
covered type of poems.

"In my own way, I write about crabs too. "
       About hiding in skin in plain sight
scurrying along
       the bottom to devour whatever scraps
       have fallen down from the careless
creatures eating above you like soul food.

"Oh yeah. Sounds different."
My great-grandmother got to write
       I had to beg and grind
crab poems. As a hobby.
       I write to breath
and they're adorable.
       my poems are ugly.
       because the beach was adorable.

Air Drums

"Drink less energy drinks.
Chemicals are not nourishment.
Carcinogens caused nodes in your chest."

Mother tells me she has breast cancer.
"We should probably drinks less energy drinks.
Apparently they're hard on your heart."

Rituals have a way of holding
on to their vice like cold
cans of tin chemo. I can't sit still

during the day after hearing
that our morning ritual hurt you. I had no clue

our caffeinated commute, and air drums
of Run to the Hills, would lead to a fight

no-one could run from. There are no breaks,
no drum solos for reprieve. No drop-offs
at school shouting, "Hey boo boo!"

on Freshman Friday. Just me, dropping
her off for the first treatment,

realizing I don't have it in me
to watch my mother die

because we can't drink energy drinks anymore.

Warning Labels: Anxiety

Symptoms include but are not limited to:
Skittishness, thoughtlessness, restlessness, restless
nights,
fun things become stressful
because you must have the most fun possible
and the stressful things become fun
because at least you feel justified in picking at your face,
biting at your nails, or pulling at your hair.

Clear capsule, filled with
People's bullshit.

Prescription: Nobody cares
about you.
Let that sink in.
Nobody
cares.

Possible medications include: Xanax, Ambien, Zoloft,
a crippling drug addiction, rusted out antique car
collection, and a notebook filled with old dreams.
Side Effects include: Jesus, name it.
You wouldn't know by the titles,
that read like the names of muses
to dead Greco-Roman philosophers,
but most of this shit will kill you.

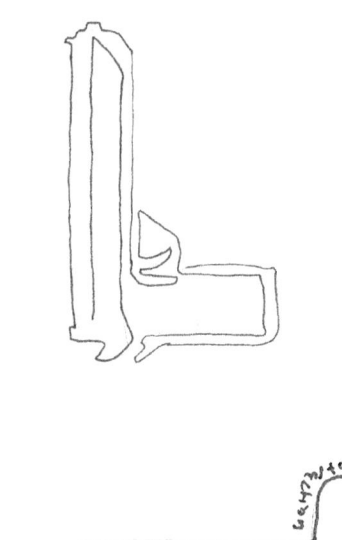

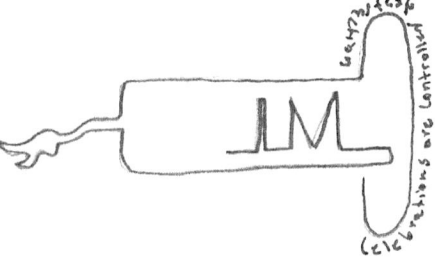

celebrations are controlled

Cold Sodas and Memories

Stress shows in the whites of Gramps' knuckles,
the tufts of hair hide the strain of holding tight
to the guilt from nuclear generations. Nana can't
remember and he can't forget. He can't forget
the small moments. He can't forget the smells.
He can't forget the sounds. He can't forget the alarms,

or the bills, or the chores, or the yard,
or the power, or the hospital, or the appointment.
When they leave he'll recall the handbag, the cooler, the backpack,
the pills, the cold sodas, the ice, the phones, the toys,
the art supplies to play with the kids
even though, "the littles" is the closest they'll have to names.

What if she forgets Gramps' name?
He can't forget to pour along the side over ice, just right,
and keep the diet cola cold because it says, "I love you"
in a way she remembers, and he can't forget.

Cans of life support

Death Feels like Science Fiction

8:25 A.M., 3/1/2017, EXT. PARKING LOT

of a local Walmart. Grabbing groceries on a family credit card.
The phone rings. My mother answers
with the volume up loud enough for me to hear.

Mom
"Your grandfather is dead."

8:17 P.M., 3/3/2017, INT. PLANE, PHOENIX

At 10,000 ft. the I-10 looks like veins on a leaf.
At 20,000 ft. the canals look like the veins in my arm.
At 30,000 ft. the city looks like a Lite-Bright.

9:00 A.M., 3/4/2017, INT. FUNERAL HOME

at the podium.
Palms wet as the world Costner sailed through,
mouth as dry as Lynch's Dune. I find no comfort
in the rose-tinted nostalgia stories of Camaros and GTOs
because for every hot-rod night of youth,
there was a night stuck, unable to move
with heads crashed down on the kitchen table,
and because for every conquest worth retelling,
there was a story trapped behind Ray's lips,
unable to escape except in small monosyllabic bursts.
But I find comfort from the physician as Gibran instructed.

1:00 P.M., 3/4/2017, INT. KITCHEN

overflowing with comfort food.
Comfort from reincarnation life cycles like Alien Chest-Busters.
Comfort from metamorphosis metaphors from molted moths and
butterflies.
Comfort from misplaced commas. The afterlife is so unsure.
Comfort from the hearty, brow beaten laughs from Ray's brother,
Ben,

that reverberate off the polished pine casket
and echo through the hollow left behind Ray's eyes.
They have the same informative tone and warmth.
I take comfort in knowing that projects can always been finished
so long as they're taken up by someone else.

10:46 P.M., 3/4/2017, INT. GRANPA RAY'S BASEMENT

Thick dust settled in the basement like it payed rent,
and musk was a squatter who never cleaned
the room or himself and binge watched
Ridley Scott discographies and Mad Max marathons
on Sci-fi because the reality channel is boring
and he can't be bored.
Because he'll notice
that air
on skin
feels
like
need
les.

7:57 P.M., 3/5/2017, INT. PLANE, INDIANAPOLIS

At 10,000 ft. the tree tops start to look like the hair
      on the newborns head,
      sat in front of me,
      silent as the grave,
      that Ray never got to meet.
At 20,000 ft. the suburbs start to look like Grandpa Ray's unfinished
train board:
      scattered houses in drawers, unbuilt models in yellowing
      boxes,
      loose line drawings of lavish plans, assorted scenery.
At 30,000 ft. the clouds roll like waves,
      and I see my Grandfather in my reflection.

Single Use Rockets

Above the top self,
tucked back in a spot
even the dust forgot,
is the toy that taught
me to shoot for the stars.
Or, at the very least,
gave me some facts:

"Press one for liftoff!"
Insert cards for Saturn, Mars, Jupiter,
the moon in all its phases and moods,
just one button to meet with her
under my medium stucco-sky.

"All systems are go!"
Lights glistening across books
of dragons, and pirates, and forgotten gods.

"All systems are-"
gone beyond plastic and glue and paint.

"All systems"
are down. The lights are out.

"All"
the batteries are gone.

It might as well have said,
"Aim for the moon and
if you miss, you land among the stars
and suffocate in the vacuum of space."

Proper Reactions to Gun Shots

There's no need to be alarmed.
You've seen it all before.

       Then:

Tell your loved ones to stay put.
Large caliber rounds aren't for small caliber people.

       Or

Make sure nobody is bleeding out
by the base of the stairs or on your porch.

       Or

You don't need those landscaping problems.
You'd rather have the blood on your hands.

       Or

When you see the shooter running,
don't say anything to anybody
because one dead black man
is better than two dead black men.

       Or

Stay vigilant until your cigarette reduces itself to ash.
After that, it's no longer your problem.

       Or

Avoid police, you probably look like the shooter.

       Then:

Go back to bed and lay still until you fall asleep
to the chirp of ghetto birds.

Unmarked Grave*

I came by the flyer from a funeral,
while weary a year later
packing up to move more memories

further away from the block we grew up on...
     where we'd hitch a ride
     deep into the suburbs
     or hop on the bus to catch
     classes we'd skip for blunts
     we'd smoke down to roaches.

I remember getting separated from the motorcade...
     like I've forgotten how he'd remind
     me of my community and how we'd
     flee using bus passes and IOUs as passports
     to privilege and full fridges.

I just missed when they put you in the ground...
     In hindsight, I could've ran
     I could've driven myself
     Instead of carpooling but collective
grief is a good excuse
to grow colder.

He's six feet deep by the back,
under the freeway, by the chain,
link fence and unkempt bushes,
about six feet over from a John Doe,

the two have matching headstones,
they too have matching headstones.

but I'll remember the syllables that formed his identity,
and the place they laid his name to rest.
I hope that I can live as he did:
defending what I love
shielding innocence.

*A version of this poem is buried at the foot of an unmarked grave. I
have no idea why I did it but it felt like the right thing to do at the time.

How I Check the Mail as a Black Man in a Red State

Step 1:
Take off the BLM shirt you've lived in
since all those videos of lives were taken.
People get irrational when they're triggered,

especially when there's an invisible trigger
on my hip, or in my pocket, or behind my back,
or in the crack of my ass,
or anywhere my hands
seem to reach.

It's best to just wear a white-tee.

Step 2:
Bring your wallet. You never know
when or how you'll need to be identified.

Luckily, years of poor nutrition
have left me with bad teeth
and a unique dental record.

On a side note:
never pick up a wallet,
we've been lynched for less.

young-ish cactus

Step 3:
Bring your keys. All your keys:
Mail key, pool key, car key, bike lock and P.O. Box.
Keys imply responsibility. Nobody was ever afraid
of a janitor but God forbid if I
have a hard time getting my box open.
Black men get a thirty second window to work a lock

before peeking the suspicion of the neighborhood watch

and if we want to be able to walk home with a bag of Skittles
it's best to avoid being seen all together.

But it's much safer to be seen in warm weather.
The heat makes people crazy

and there is some truth to safety in numbers
but it assumes the group isn't a lynch mob.

Step 4:

Be quick.
You own nothing and everything

until you are inside. Every raggedy backpack is yours
and every package is too rich for your blood.

Eye contact and idle conversation is a privilege
that doesn't extend past the bedroom or the dinner table
unless being served a warrant or being shot
8 times while in bed for your boyfriend's parcel.

Step 5:

Pray it's Sunday or do it all again.

A Real Quick Trip

"I've got to be honest: I kind of like the statues,
even the racist ones." At least that
is what the gas station clerk told me.
I wanted caffeine so I could get back to grind my game,
but he insisted on selling his history
like a cheap salesman trying to lease the lemon on the lot.

I said, "I kind of like them too. They remind me of my place,
or at least where you'd want me: at your feet,
or just within sight, but at an arm's reach."
or, I wish I'd said that.

Their heroes are our villains, their feast means
our famine, their Utopia is my waking nightmare.

I wish I had beat my chest and flashed
my whole asshole, like all "those monkeys
at the protests."

In that moment, I didn't share a damn thing.

Because, I've got to be honest.
I kind of like the statues. Even the racist ones.

They point like a way finder in a video game
towards an objective I'm not a high enough level to deal
with yet but best believe when I find the armor I need
I'll die on that fucking hill,
a monument to poplar trees.

But I didn't say any of that. I didn't say anything at all.
I just listened to his podcast punch me while it played.
I listened when he told me to learn about his lineage
and spewed a bunch of facts he "bet I didn't know."

But what he didn't know is
I kind of like the statues.

"Black" Comedy

"What's the loneliest day?
in a black neighborhood."
       Fuck, gotta get my funny face on.
"Father's Day."

I laughed the first five times
as a freshmen. Once some seniors
and teammates "joke" enough,
and chase you around with a noose,
gallows humor becomes the go-to.

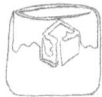

In hindsight, I'd re-write the moment some.
Add in a 'Fuck you' for good measure,
register the hazing as a hate crime as it happens.
But it always starts with jokes and code

switching is easier than fighting words. Shame
is safer than crossing swords and pissing
into the wind I have to sit in.

I'd re-write the joke a bit,
"What's the most lonely day in suburbia?
Today."

A Pictures Worth for Floyd

A close up of a mouth gasping for fluid and pleading for mercy. An umbilical cord wrapped around a throat squeezing tight and wheezing. Lips cracked like California fault lines. The creases filled with blood from chapped corners signaling vitamin deficiencies from before this meeting. Teeth stained from use and chipped from being used as tools. Plague filled in the gaps between where floss should've been but there's no time to floss in between shifts or while on the grind. Missing molars where metal ones could've taken their place. Maybe they would've gotten replaced eventually. They'll stay broken now. Asphalt pressed into the sides of his eyes by where the brow begins to taper off. Sirens echo red off the tears in the mud color iris looking toward home but blocked by a knee on a neck. In brief moments of relief, his face lifted up to let the pain pass underneath it. But the time spent against the ground forced the small loose pebbles to press into his face. These would be the most superficial wounds. Streets are hottest during midday and it was afternoon. Or more precisely, after high-noon. That's when lynchings take place in movies. When deputies take in the runaway. Except, he hadn't runaway. I guess it doesn't matter in a system as old as slavery that still polices as such. And one that holds grudges. Grudges that can be pulled up on newscasts and broadcast on demand should we be murdered. They did it for him. Those videos preceded these photos. And that was by design. This moment was by design. This moment had a grudge, it always does, like an ex-boyfriend that looks similar and made the attacking, or "responding," officer feel like a cuck, or advice from a police chief who lost out on that promotion to "affirmative action" so he recites crime statistics from r/TheDonald. I guess if it walks like a duck and quacks like a duck then it's probably a fucking racist and if it walks like racist and incites violence then it's a cop. Or police officer. We've got to be respectful even when there's a knee on our necks. "Stop resisting" should be reclassified as fighting words. They imply a fight is already occurring even when just resting like a heartbeat that will hiccup when "stop resisting" starts meaning "stop breathing". "Stop breathing and comply," sounds a lot more accurate to expectations. Expectations like prejudice. Expectations like the sun will come up tomorrow. And the sun did come up that morning. It shown down on the scene. It heated the pavement until it could cook and egg. It was instead used to cook a face and evaporate tears as they fell and rolled down. Tears trickled past an Adams apple that may have been as big as his sons. I guess they'll never know. Tears rolled down to saturate a collapsed chest with a murderer standing on it. A murderer who may as well have been named Cain. A chest with a heart that will likely be blamed despite not knowing its content. A heart that will be given birth defects or murmurs or croaks or previous conditions other than stuck under the boot of a Klansmen with a badge bashing up against ventricles. The number one 'widow maker' in black neighborhoods isn't a heart attack but an attack on the heart. A heart heavy with the weights of fatherhood, of brotherhood, of servitude to a system that would steal his breath. Behind that heart was a back where burden used to rest but instead there was a man sitting on it like there was a fucking shade tree, like an apple may fall on his head and give him the novel idea not to be a murderous asshole. But of course nothing fell from the sky. There were no miracles. God did not smite him and neither did his partner and neither did the spectators because fear is a hell of a motivator and it could have just as easily been any one of us sent to hell as a motivator. So to keep it from being one of us we filmed and took photos because it can't be us anymore. Maybe they would believe us when they see this. Even though this is routine, this is expected, this is the norm, this is the banality of evil. Our hands are clasped by it. Hands clasped and wrapped like swine swung up and ready for a fire. Hands bound but somehow they are still weapons. Everywhere black skin extends is a weapon to white men. This skin was no different but this skin is unique because it was seen. Most died in the credits or in the footnotes or as black marks on records that could easily be erased. But we can't erase a face we've seen. And we can't dream about faces that haven't been in our lives. I'm glad I replay this scene over and over again when I close my eyes. Or I might have looked away. And I can't look away this time because Floyd looked just like my father, and my brother, and my uncles, and my O.G.s who fed me. He looked just like our friends and our family and our neighbors and we couldn't look away as they were taken from us. Taken away and wiped clean like dirty elbows soaked in spit because there wasn't enough lotion at home. Elbows bloodied and scrapped, knees the same. Ashy enough to get torn up at the lunch table but getting bullied to the pavement would take the coco butter of anyone's skin. The knee on his neck isn't ashy. White people don't get ashy and it's hard to be exposed in military surplus garbs. The knee on his neck isn't trembling. It is exactly where it wants to be: crushing life. The spectators aren't helping because they're exactly where they need to be: watching it die.

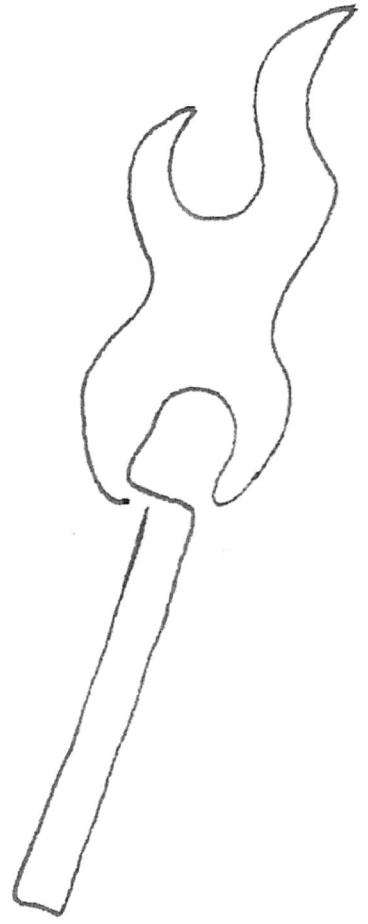

Batman for Charity

There's no Batman in my borough
(If Arizona had enough culture
to have those) but we have a few
dudes named Bruce or something
that lead militias and mess
with Mexicans. If Batman lived near me

he'd probably just beat up brown people.
He'd probably wear a Sherriff's badge
for protection and project
an extra sus sign into the sky.

He'd probably go to the same temple,
or church as the local oligarchy
and laugh with the fat cats.
The Joker would be a talking head,
and the news would say they're best friends.

There is no Superman in my city,
and if there were, he'd be an alien,
an illegal one, by Batman's measure.
Maybe that's why they've always had beef.

We do have Lex Luthor though.
He gentrified my block a year ago
and called it progress. Took out all
the color and said it was cleaner.
It looked better this way

And if there was a Wonder Woman
around the way, she definitely moved
the day the catcalling graduated to assault.

Maybe on Paradise Island, there was more
for mothers than sons without fathers.
Maybe the Amazons were worth fighting for.

There are no heroes in my hood. Just people
working for their peace of earth.

Warning Labels: Depression

Symptoms include but are not limited to:
an intense sadness
at things as trivial as the dust at the end of a bag of potato
chips.
Nobody eats the crumbs.

Rigged white tablet,
that sticks to the uvula
as it goes down. Mmm,
delicious.

Prescription: Get the fuck
out of that cold ass room.

Possible medications include: Zoloft, Lexapro, Cymbalta,
Prozac, Celexa, Wellbutrin, Abilify, and the loud clap of
a .45 round passing through your eardrum and into your
brain. Or a puppy.
Side effects include: increased mood swings, dry mouth,
difficulty swallowing, diarrhea, vomiting, and the loud
clap of a .45 passing through your ear drum and into your
brain.

28

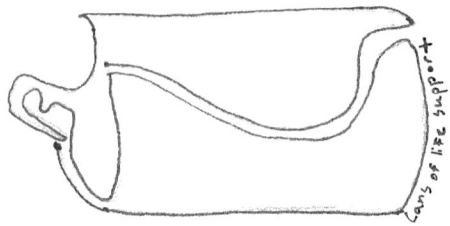

cans of life support

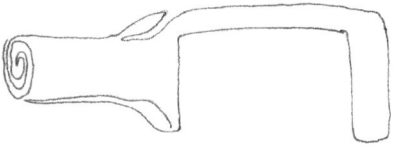

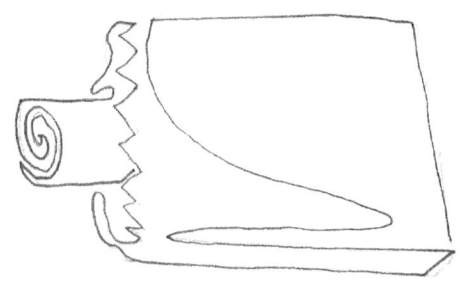

Clayton Bigsby and the 4th Stage

I'd never cried for my people
or come to terms with being
as I am where I am. While
the spine of Malcolm X was broken
and tattered in my back pocket,
plastered with pain from paper cuts of pages
turned furiously. Maybe it was misplaced.

Perhaps I can be less of what I am
and in exchange my place will change.
Replace my slang with speech and
maybe I'd be allowed to speak. Not preach,
but bellow and yell from low in my chest.

I'd never cried for my people until Chapelle
showed me what I'd known: "Any black man
that survives is my goddamn hero."
I had been Bigsby: blind and belligerent,
wearing white robes to malign my melanin
and align with lies I'd read in class and on screen.

Bigsby is one truth from, "all of Nigerdom."
I am what I am: a black man in America.
and a villain to the rest of them.

Window Shopping

Pick a shade of white or grey,
something cool and neutral to go
with all that color. Try it on,
take a number, find your place

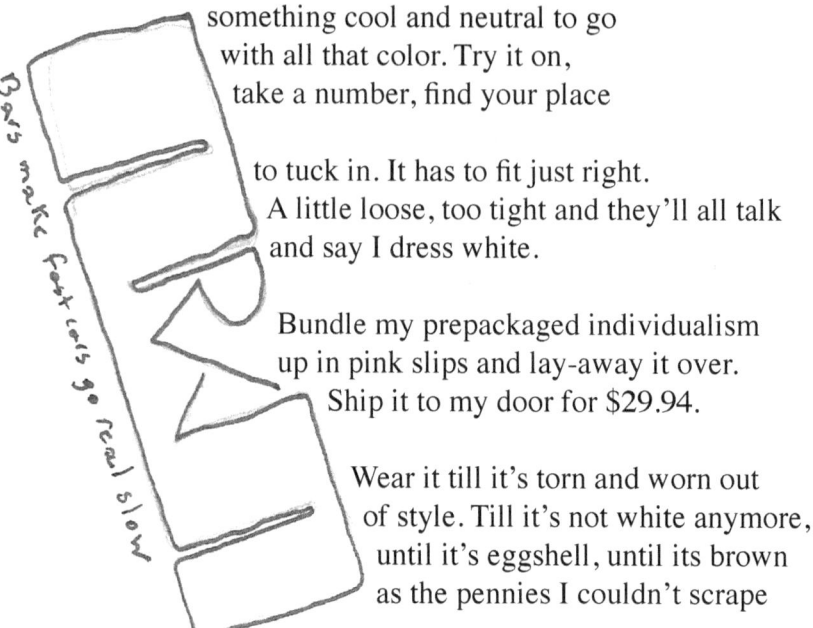

to tuck in. It has to fit just right.
A little loose, too tight and they'll all talk
and say I dress white.

Bundle my prepackaged individualism
up in pink slips and lay-away it over.
Ship it to my door for $29.94.

Wear it till it's torn and worn out
of style. Till it's not white anymore,
until it's eggshell, until its brown
as the pennies I couldn't scrape

across a porcelain toy. Bank
account overdraft oversized logo

on my torso. Can't afford to be black
shopping from the clearance rack.

Office Supply

Drop me in a vat of white-off.
Erase me and make me invisible

Strip the ink from my soul
and make me mute to the eye
that will be my super power.

No need to cross the street
faster and faster as my dreads grow

No need to eyeball me through
the store. You won't even know

I'm there. A light knot tied
from stripped silk will be the only thing
holding me back in an interview.

Maybe it'd be a meritocracy for me
if I was The Invisible Man,

or maybe a white man,

or even a man at all.

Wholesome masculinity is a gift from

No Insecure Contestants

I want to be as brave as Rupaul:
brash and bold as a bad bitch,

an unapologetic type of presence,
and one I've never understood.

Peacocks profoundly confound me
because they are proud. They wear plumage

and I have none of which to speak. Who am I
to be loud when I have no voice? Who am I

to dare to be colorful when I've sinned
against the melanin in my skin? Who am I

to be as anyone when I can barely be
as myself?

The Third Verse

I've covered up my heart
for far too long, in short
bursts of pediatric patriotism,
while standing up to salute people
who would rather see me on my knees.
Unless, it is during their song,
or it is my choice to be there
for prayer, or for protests, or to plead

that this is my nation, and it's my anthem, too.
The first and second verses say as much about me
as the third does about them. A nation built on slaves
hides its past in childish games like invisible pens,
missing lyrics in fight themes and National Anthems.
But the tune I'm being asked to sing from the heart
erased the verses that included me:

being hunted with dogs like a bitch. I heard them
in stadiums and classrooms, and I studied their echoes.
"No refuge could save" any slave from their freedom.
Red, White, and green tidal waves of liberty
as secure as Colin Capernick's career,
as American as apple pie:
"the terror of flight or the gloom of the grave."

White People Shit

At least Elvis would let me shine his shoes.
It's a job, right?
He'd probably prefer I wear gloves like Mickey Mouse,
white to match ivory keys I wanted to learn to play
before Ed said the piano was white people shit.
So, I stripped chicken skins from drumsticks
snapped snares and crashed cymbals of Star Wars themes
in suburbs whitewashed down to white walled churches
complete with speed balls withdrawn from Adderall.
Scripts for shit you don't need. That's some white people shit.
I pawned Hendrix guitar riffs for pencil tip taps and palm slaps
on gym bleachers, basketball bounce bass,
and sixteen bars from whoever had heart.
I sat on my hands and chewed my cheek,
something white people sure as shit wouldn't do,
because my voice was white people shit.
I got down on bare knees and brought my voice to the floor,
prayed to God, Allah, Yahweh, and Jehovah for the Mother
tongue to return, for new words to split my tongue
blister and callous over and spit venom.
But prayer is white people shit. My people sing.
I never learned to speak because I saw
too many brown people pile in wood-stained pews,
preach from white bibles, and praise a white Jesus:
a little Constantinople, a bit of Odin's sun.
I guess God is white people shit.

Black as a Moor Bruise

The curriculum map is missing
sections and legends set in
boundaries and borders beyond,
the one point that apparently matters:
the West.

My books tell me the West is unmatched.
unless you move to the margins
where there is some Moor knowledge
or glance at the glossary
where the lists and terms always cite
Africa and Asia: for markets, for cities,
for science, for math, for trade, for language.
Take a peek at the captions
where there is vibrancy and color

even though the photo is in black and white,
remember the rhythms of the songs
does not belong trapped in black or white
ink and enshrined in numerals.
Remember the page numbers
like longitudes and latitudes
moving past pictures:

A black bust of a black king
chest out, gilded and proud
as all get out. Proud as we
never learned to be. Add to me

like algebra and reduce this cipher
down to its chemistry. Chart its course
among the stars we count and count on not
knowing about how Europe got that bruise
under its eye or how its jaw got crooked.

Taught since we were reared to revere
Revere's ride but never reminded of our ride,
our regality, "their horses were as fire,
their faces black as pitch, their eyes
shone like burning candles,
their horse were swift."

Stand as tall and stiff as the bust
draped in violet velvet and gold
and cased in copper with a burgundy
bruise right under our right eye.

Appointment with the Physician

INT., PSYCH. OFFICE, AFTERNOON
Modified breakroom, shades drawn, long and lean Ikea love seat, ceiling high filing cabinets, One Che-weenie, assorted fidget toys lit by computer screens.
Outside the window a wood pecker assaults a cactus for its fruit, a neighbor peeks inside looking to catch a glimpse of some crazy but is disappointed to just see me.

Physician
I've tallied your scores. Let's discuss the results some more.

Self
Thank god, that's what I'm here for.

Physician
What do you think anxiety is?

Self
Anxiety is chain-smoking,
in an office parking lot, while stray petals rain
into the bed of a beaten down pick up,
crushing smoldering shorts into a silo filled with tar,
shuffling salmon papers from ash covered folders,
adjusting test scores, trying to change who I am,
until just before this appointment.

Physician
Tell me more.

Self
Anxiety is constantly checking
for a bus that is always late
and keeping two copies of you-
r identification besides backups
of registration, not for a gun,

rights need not apply. Anxiety
is reading resume requirements as
"need not apply." Anxiety is constant
over-spending, over-eating, over-saving, over-grinding,
For a day when enough isn't enough.

Physician
What about depression?

Self
What about it? Depression is
a balmy cocoon in a frigid room
the sun can't reach, but the moon can.

Physician
Are you familiar with ADHD?

Self
I'm familiar with perpetually putting together a septillion-piece puzzle
and frantically fumbling for the final piece:
a small section of stormy skies,
showing the sun just starting to peak
through holes in the clouds as it rises in the sky.
But the last piece isn't in the box
or under the mattress by an old sock or stuck
in the couch, next to extra cheddar Goldfish crumbs,
and if I could just...

...focus for long enough to remember
where it went, the picture would be complete.

Physician
Good news, we have pills for that.

Self
For your check that's all good and well
But I'd rather not take pills that kill

I've escaped that hell
And I'd rather not go back.

Physician
What else has brought you
to need
help.

Self
There's an imposter in my flesh.
It thinks like me, moves as me,
steals my breath as its own.
It pushes fear from my palms
Till they're slick from work
and worse for wear. The imposter
beats at my chest like it's got a warrant,
unitl the rhythm moves two beats too fast.
It tells me that I am the fly in the milk
and the rust on the kettle. It says
I can't speak until I can say my name
in the tounge of my home, that I do not know
the soil and concrete from where I was grown
or hold tight tales from old kinfolk I couldn't have know.
It holds me accountable for sins unseen,
insvisible boundaries crossed, rules not listed,
and words left unspoken.

Physician
What do you want
from your healing?

Self
I want to move like my mirror image.
I want to look like my reflection.
I want to be my shadow.

Physician

Why is it better to be
your shadow than yourself?

Self
My shadow has seen the best of me
The rest is uncertain. Shadows are sure
and patient. They wait
to move until placed on the path
perfect to keep their shape
with fingers reaching across the day
to pull the sky toward them slowly
revealing all that was still. I run
from my shadow, still too precarious to stop,
afraid that if it catches me,
I will fall in.

Capsules are full of room to chill with less bills.

Warning Labels: ADHD

Symptoms include but are not limited to: disassociation, limited attention span, difficulty recalling information and

Round Orange Tablet. Wish it tasted like Tang. Remember that stuff?

Prescription: Find the missing puzzle piece.
Hint: It's in your hand.

Possible medications include, but are not limited to: Adderall, Ritalin, Concerta, Vyvanse, Clonidine, Strattera, Provigil, Wellbutrin

Side Effects include but are not limited to: vomiting, nausea, difficulty swallowing, chest pains, diarrhea, constipation, depression, suicide, weight gain, weight loss, acne, and loss of appetite.

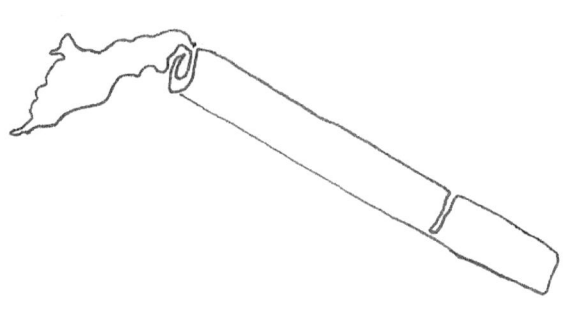

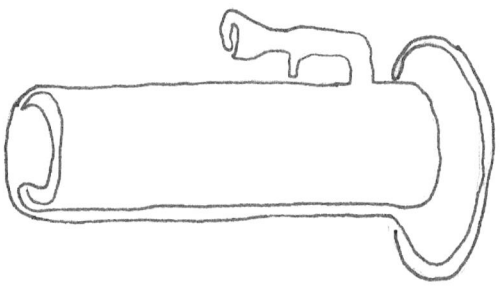

At America's Diner on Acid

I asked for her true name.
"I have had many names:
Enso, Ouroboros, Infiniti;
but respond to only one
that has no earthly tongue,"
she hissed to me
over stale coffee,
sourdough and spoiled eggs,
served sunny-side down
with flakes from a fluorine sign.
I asked for her true name.
Instead, I was
lead while idle,
past fields
of circus tents,
the door to each open
wider than the last.
Furthur through,
rows of slot machines
ring, promising freedom
as gleaming nuggets
of temptation. I sat
in a line to a queue
for an interview where
I asked for her true name.

Mythos of the Modern Weed-Man

"This shit is crazy fam. The pandy had a designer plan,"
said the friendly neighborhood weed-man,

"By some September, the aliens arrive fashionably late
and we'll be so disgusted by their racism, we'll cancel them,
alongside the dolphins for their rapes in the 60's,
which will drive them under sea where Minoan tech
will give rise to a new-age master race of pedophile
semi-aquatic reptilians that will align the planets
with daddy Trump's hairline and overthrow
the pizza peddling overlords."

He's seen it all written in whispers
scrawled across message board walls:
the prophecy of the Coke can,
the Kubrick Moon sham,
the subliminal army of 4-chan
sweats sworn to form into Zords.

At least someone has a plan.
Nothing can surprise me anymore
after the friendly neighborhood weed-man.

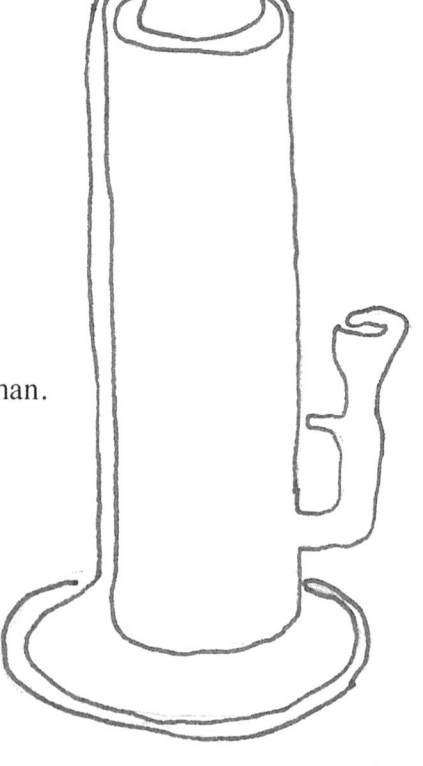

Illuminate Waffle

I want an Illuminati Waffle
piled high with cream
whipped into a bent upright position
cowering into submission in houses
like caves cresting with butter and syrup
a sweet reprieve in pockets of tender joy.

Next to that, throw in some bacon
sliced thin, and cooked crispy.
Not peasant pig that lives in its shit
and eats worse, but pork
that was pampered with painted nails
and air conditioning. Gimme one that remembers
comfort before it was cured, pulled, and smoked.

Throw on some eggs. Not from chickens
but from quails. I want to destroy innocence.
Like inner city experiments, fertilization seasoned
with syphilis and some CIA corner store crack spices.
Render it all down to its essential fats.

As a matter of fact, top that undeveloped breast with syrup
thick as the nectar of our mother. Keystone XL
flavored, leaking out of the side while you pour
like Denny's dispensers table-top spills.

Mmm mmm, that good ole' Americana
piled high like bodies.
My manifest destiny, a packed plate
of New World short-Orders.
Maybe I'll finally feel full.

Plausible Deniability and Status Feeds

News feed filled with conspiracy theory
and pictures of people's ugly offspring.
A bunch of shit
I don't want to know.

I don't want to know about a disabled kid being bullied
with a coat hanger in his rectum
because his father got him a red hat for the wrong candidate.

I don't want to know about the kids burning
to death from the inside in Aleppo.
Gas is a cruel mistress, a dominatrix, and
I like the way she hurts me.
It smells bittersweet like my freedoms.

I don't want to know about the rape game.
I don't want to know that hordes of Brazilian men corner women
and rape them, while the others form a circle to protect
the participants and keep them safe from harm.

I don't want to know what an aborted fetus looks like
because women need their reproductive rights,
but a placenta covered fetal corpse is instinctually distressing.

I don't want to know "never gain"
was a lie, and Muslims make cell phones
and shoes in the same rooms
where they were forcibly sterilized.

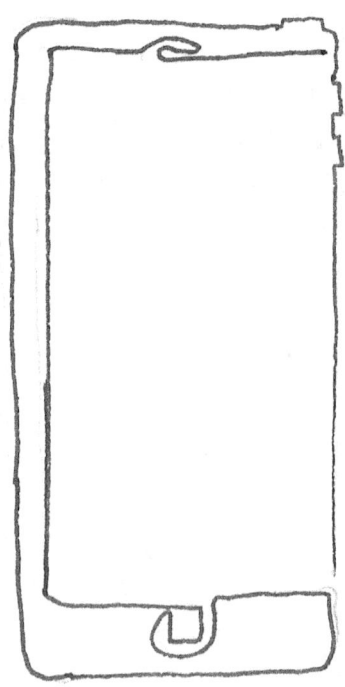

I don't want to know about the kidnappings,
even if it might be someone I know.
It is just too much stress,

and I can't do anything about anything
from my computer screen but throw donations
in measly increments laundered through gasoline-and-
concentration-camp-supporting-war-bond-buying big banks.

I don't want to know,
because life is hard enough as it is.
I don't want to know,
because if I knew, then I would have to act,
and likes don't feel appropriate.

Friend Requests

Two friends I haven't seen in years,
a classmate that somehow found my profile,
a bot account promising free sex in my area,
the last from my father, Ken.

I dread having to break the ice
with old friends, ever since I met Ken
once, two families ago.
He wanted to play catch,
I wanted to play catch-up.
He has a different name now
that he is a proud Muslim
and no longer a slave. I didn't have
the eggshell basketball he got me,
even though I wanted it,
but I kept the words
he never meant to give me:
bastard, black sheep. I learned young
when he beat my ass.
My hands still sweat
when I play Mortal Kombat.

My peers who found me online
probably know more about me
than my father. I wanted to respond with a list
of some of the highlights Ken missed:
my first steps, my first words, my first fight,
or any firsts for that matter,
my family's cheers echoing off steel bleachers,
the stench of bleach, sweat, and blood
wafting from wrestling mats to a bench,
the hollow ting of a baton bouncing off a track,

the silence when I fumbled
over my speech in Decathlon
and lost a medal for my team,
or my angry cries
when I got screwed trading
my holographic Superman comic
for a crumbled copy of The Hobbit.

I wonder if I should shoot him a DM
to tell him what I've learned
from my mother, instead of him
teaching me to be
a man. Pics of me
learning to pee with Fruit Loops
floating in the final flush
of a decades old, piss-stained bowl.
A slide show of how to use a condom
on a spoiled, bruised banana
bought with a Texaco credit card.
A close-up of my face
frozen
when a bald man in a mall
calls me a nigger
and I ask
my lily-white mother
what a nigger is.

I accept Ken's request--
at least we played catch-- and respond,
"Sorry it took so long to get back to you."

Rain Checks

Corrupted data looks like missing friends
in photos. New frames that have cut me out
of my own past. Data decays as it's used,

and maybe I've worn it down to digits,
to a random number in a friends count.
The memories I lost quantified in beats
missed and harmonies skipped. Bytes

and bits of myself destroyed through misuse
that I can scarcely remember

like song lyrics I stumble signing
rain checks never cashed
and pictures cropped by decay.

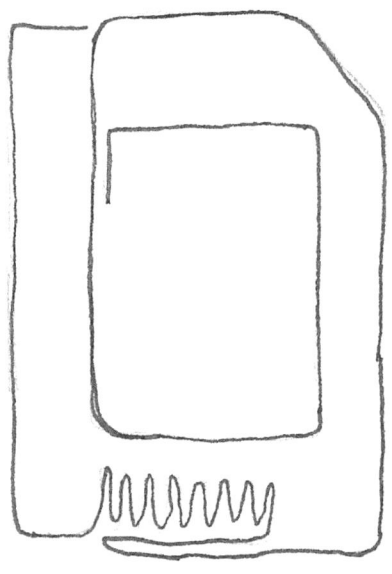

Everything but the Kitchen Sink

Pots, pans, spatulas,
       wet with no stick
       caked in crusted remnants
       of half-assed, piss drunk
       gothic cupcake cooking experiments
plates, bowls, silverware,
       valleys, canyons, and Mesas
       for the ridges of chips,
       mountains of crusts,
       fungus flowering on fruit
deep bourbon brown bowl,
       greased slick and shiny
       from movie and popcorn
       rainy day afternoons
       sleeping with eyes open
blunt ash, bourbon stained shot glass,
       from birthdays spent alone
       and nights in solitary
       being shouted at
       in silence, still as dry bones
second hand wood board, serrated butcher's knife,
       jagged as a Welsh cliffside
       from where I cut
       kush colored key limes
       and smashed wilted mint
bent whisk, balled up napkins,
       covered in batter
       from the Log Cabin

pancakes that slopped

up the Moscow Mules

crumpled rags, repurposed grocery bags, strainer with dry macaroni,

to seep up the vomit

on my porch, soaked in acid

shades of sherbet orange

glow stick gut green

garbage disposal blades,

and biomes that have grown alone.

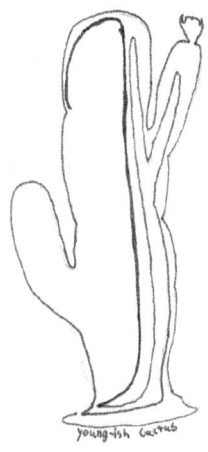

young-ish cactus

wholesome masculinity is a gift from a father

Acknowledgment

"Not at all. It's a fake confessional. I'm not really confessing. The fact that I confess to be a fraud is a fraud. It is just as deliberate & manipulative as that. No I think I'm "absolutely genuine"—that's a lie! I never tell the truth." - Orson Welles on Art as Confession in *My Lunches with Orson*

Author's Note

This book contains noncontigous line drawings intended to represent how the decisions of our past paint the course of our present and shape our future.

Marcus Sterling Campbell is a poet and film enthusiast from Phoenix, Arizona. Graduating from Mesa Community College, he received a high distinction in Creative Writing, along with degrees in Journalism and General Studies. He is a Vortex Award winner and has placed in several writing contests within the Mesa community. Marcus sweats when he writes and while growing his Magic collection. His work can be found scattered across the web or @marcus_s_campbell on social media.

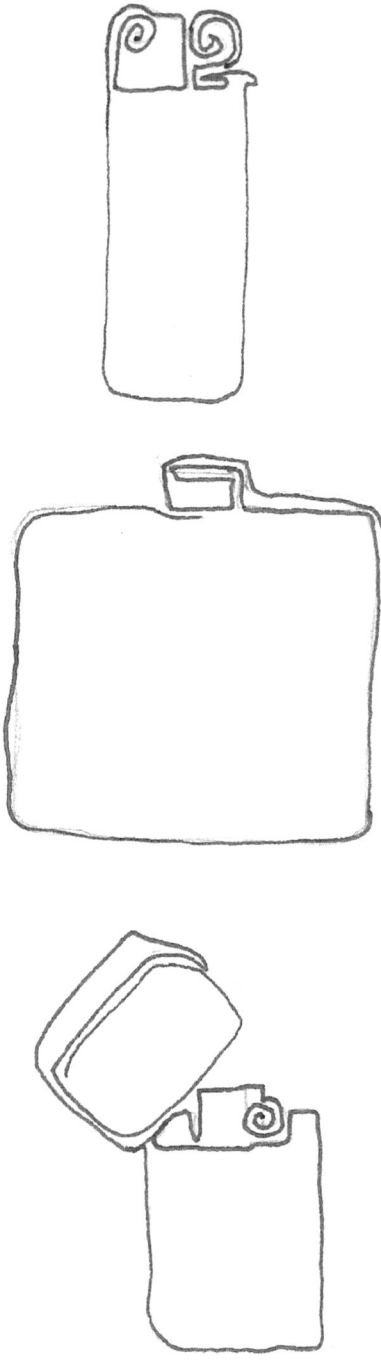

For best experience, please rotate book 180° before continuing.

www.ingramcontent.com/pod-product-compliance
Lightning Source LLC
Chambersburg PA
CBHW070942250626
47159CB00009B/3350

My Identity as a Stereotypical Side Character
(Cold Sodas)
Published by Brick Cave Books
All rights reserved

Illustrations by Marcus Campbell
Interior Book Design and Layout by Brick Cave Books
Production Services and Support by John Blair

Cover art: ©2022 Marcus Campbell

Printed in the United States of America

Brick Cave Media
brickcavebooks.com

Cold Sodas

Stories by
Marcus S. Campbell

Brick Cave Media
brickcavebooks.com

Table of Contents

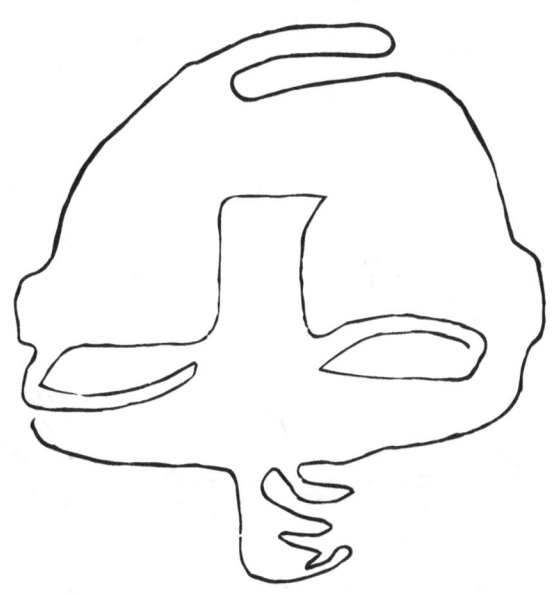

Dedication

Thank you, my brothers.

Cold Sodas

The usual cornucopia and chorus of sounds, sights, and smells pulled Michael toward home like a tide to shore. Ms. Nikki's truck tires rolled with percussive precision over the uneven pavement of his street. Neighbors had already started cooking and backyard barbeques burned big and beautiful and pushed bellows of mesquite smoke down the street.

A group of kids sat around the above ground electrical box in a circle with their backs to the street. Smoke with a different smell snuck its way out from between them and into the window of the truck. Teenagers yelled at each other on the basketball court across the street. The rumblings of a fight could be heard bubbling like bass beneath the blaring Banda music spilled from the houses. The truck pulled into the drive way.

Michael swung his door open and shut using every muscle on his right side. The strap of his backpack shifted off his slender shoulder and into the sweaty crook of his elbow. He didn't bother slinging it back again. Instead, he hustled to the door ahead of Ms. Nikki while she rummaged through the truck.

Ms. Nikki gathered her sodas and her purse. She picked at the top of her wig with an anxious grit that slowly tuned into relief before the wig slipped and became an annoyance again. Michael picked up the fake rock, pulled out the spare key hidden within, and unlocked the door. He waited patiently until Ms. Nikki walked inside and then replaced the key. Ms. Nikki went immediately to the bathroom.

Michael put his backpack on the hook and turned to lock the front door. Zoey leapt up to greet him. The jolt made Michael's feet shift in his poorly tied basketball shoes until he caught himself on the ball of his sole via

the hole through which his sock peeked out.

Michael swept Zoey's paws from his legs and wiped off his khaki uniform. Mud from Zoey's paws streaked down the center of his pants legs near the starched crease. Michael slid on his socks to the kitchen, grabbed a Tupperware container from the cupboard and dropped dog food into a ceramic bowl.

Stretching up onto his tippy toes, he investigated the top shelf of the fridge. Food was meticulously organized by type and freshness: sodas on top, then that week's leftovers, then meats and cheeses, dairy and water jugs on the bottom shelf, and fruits and veggies underneath.

Using small hops, he flicked the sodas with the tips of his fingers. He shuffled over to the pantry and grabbed four diet sodas, went back to the fridge and placed three diet sodas on the top shelf. As he loaded the fourth soda into the freezer, something shattered in the bathroom.

Zoey ran toward the bathroom with reckless abandon. Michael raced after her and managed to grab her around the neck, by the collar, and hold her back as he waited outside the bathroom.

"Are you okay, Ms. Nikki?" he asked with buckling knees and a brittle voice. He had never known Ms. Nikki to make a mess or break things. As far as Michael was concerned she might have transformed into a monster behind that door.

"Yes, buddy. You can come in."

"Are you not going number one or two?'

"No, buddy," Ms. Nikki said with a fake chortle.

Michael pushed the door open slowly.

Ms. Nikki stood with her palms on the ceramic tiled countertop and her head hanging over the sink basin. She had already changed into her immaculate nightly leisure clothes: a dizzying Technicolor sweatshirt with matching sneakers.

3

Ordinarily, the bathroom was spotless except for a pair of false eyelashes laid on the edge of the sink or small make-up spots on the stem of the faucet. This time the bathroom was different.

Products sprawled all over the sink in a threatening number of vials, jars and aerosols. A fake face taunted Michael with an expressionless gaze. On top of its head was a mountain of hair just crooked enough to remove the intimidation of the disembodied head. The bowl of the sink was laden with hair and chunks of glass. The mass manufactured plastic remnants of a hand mirror framed the wads of brittle hair and shards of glass in the sink.

"Oh shit." Michael's eyes widened, forcing his forehead to wrinkle, and tracked from the sink to Ms. Nikki's face. "I'm sorry, I didn't mean it."

"You didn't mean it? Or you didn't mean to say it?" said Ms. Nikki holding back a laugh.

"Uh, I don't know."

"You get a pass this time. 'Oh shit' is definitely the right response," she said from under a reluctant gin.

"What happened?"

Zoey yanked at Michael's arm, and whined, her nose twitched toward the sink. Ms. Nikki's sullen expression passed over to Zoe and she patted her on the head.

"The new doctor appointments make my hair fall out, buddy."

"Oh, I thought you weren't sick no more."

Ms. Nikki slowly gathered herself and began to clean the sink. "I'm only a little sick now but you can't kill cancer easy. You have to cut it out first and then make sure it never comes back."

"So, this is the 'never comes back' part?"

"Yeah, buddy."

"Will you be sick forever?"

"I'm not sure," said Ms. Nikki, the last remaining energy in her breath winding down to a whisper.

She finished cleaning the sink, took Michael by the hand and led him to the living room. She sat down on the couch and looked up at him. She inhaled deep through her nose and exhaled hard in his direction.

"Eww, Ms. Nikki. Your breath smells gross."

Ms. Nikki took another deep breath before she responded. "Sorry, baby. I always do my best."

A loud concussive pop rang out from the kitchen. Zoey sprinted toward the kitchen this time with a Chihuahua in tow. Ms. Nikki grabbed Michael's arm. Michael's breath stopped, but his heart ran as fast as the Chihuahua's legs. He knew what the explosion was.

"Oh no," Michael shouted. He popped off the couch, ripped free from Ms. Nikki's startled vice grip, and dashed toward the kitchen.

"Michael," shouted Ms. Nikki. "What did you do?"

"Oh no," Michael said again from the door of the freezer in the kitchen. "I think it exploded," he bellowed toward the couch in the living room.

"No need to yell," said Ms. Nikki as she stumbled into the kitchen. Michael jumped again. He'd always been squirrelly, but that was one jump scare too many.

"Sorry, baby." Ms. Nikki looked over the soda can carcass littering the freezer. Michael stepped back from his mess, expecting to be chastised for his carelessness. Frozen soda sat in the ice tray. The cold plastic walls had been redecorated using a high gloss yellow in a post-modern style. Slush pooled in small pockets on the racks.

5

"Did you put a soda in the freezer for me, baby?"

"Yeah, cause you said the other day that you like it to be kind of slushy."

"Thank you, baby," said Ms. Nikki with eyes as messy as the freezer.

Ms. Nikki stretched her arms around Michael and held him for what seemed like an eternity. He didn't bother trying to escape. He patted her back with the familiar rhythm of the comfortably uncomfortable.

Ms. Nikki's phone went off, and Michael went to grab it.

"Who is it, baby?" asked Ms. Nikki as she whipped her eyes.

"It's Marco," said Michael as he handed the phone to Ms. Nikki. "Am I allowed to call Marco my brother?"

"Of course you are, baby. I don't think he'd mind at all," said Ms. Nikki taking the phone. "Can you pick up your mess please, baby?"

Cleaning up the freezer was no small chore. Ms. Nikki de-briefed her son on the treatments while Michael scrubbed the plastic with thin paper towels. Holes kept tearing in the sheets, plunging Michael's fingers into the ice box. Michael decided to cut his losses and dump the ice into the sink. He finished by placing a new soda into the freezer. This time, he set a timer on the microwave before heading into to the living room.

Michael grabbed the furry blanket and the pillows, and handed them to Ms.Nikki while she talked on the phone. Once the timer went off, he placed a new soda down on the coffee table in front of Ms. Nikki and began to fidget on the rug. Michael's feet slid over the vacuum lines in the carpet. Ms. Nikki stopped talking.

Ms. Nikki handed the phone to Michael with an earnest wiggle. Michael's face lit up as he took his turn.

"Hi, Marco. Can we play Battles Royale?" he asked. "I've been practicing. I got three kills yesterday, and one was a headshot."

"I have to work right now, bud, but we can play tonight if you get your brainwork done."

Michael pulled his gaming chair from beside the movie case to the center of the living room. He positioned himself in crisscross applesauce.

"I did it at day care, and that's good cause Ms. Nikki doesn't feel good."

"Yeah. That's what I wanted to talk about buddy."

"Mhm, her hair is all over the bathroom. Like in that one movie with the girl."

Michael powered on his Game-Station, turned on the TV, and selected Battles Royale from the menu.

"Yeah bud." Marco's voice was not just tired, but depleted and broken. "Thank you for taking care of our mom when I can't."

"It was just a cold soda. No big deal." said Michael with the casual ease of childhood. If happiness had a pitch or a tone, then that was it.

"It is, bud. Sometimes a cold soda is just what the doctor ordered."

"The Pump"

Michael sat in the middle of class with his feet tucked under his butt. His head lay on the desk. Pools of drool formed around the dried out corners of his mouth. Michael groaned.

"Michael, please wake up," said his teacher. "Michael!"

Michael groaned in response. His teacher walked over to his desk and shook his shoulder.

"Wake up, Michael. Or you're going to the principal's office."

Michael slowly lifted his head. As he peeled his face off the linoleum of his desk, a string of drool followed him and attached to the small dimple between his nose and mouth.

"I'm not"

Before Michael could finish his sentence, a stream of recycled Frost- ed Flakes beat him to the punch. A waterfall of full fat dairy milk and half-digested corn meal flapped onto the floor. Michael quickly filled his teachers' shoes and doused his own shirt in the toxic cement.

Michael began to cry.

"Someone take him to the nurse's office now."

...

Ms. Nikki sat with the needle buried deep within her arm. A long tube

11

ran from her pearlescent skin up to a bag filled with a slow-moving, viscous fluid. The walls of the room were bare except for a whiteboard that displayed the names of nurses and staff on call with their access numbers.

Ms. Nikki swung her legs from the hospital bed, and her booties slid onto the tile. She pulled the I.V. pole to her side and sat up. Using her phone, she dialed for her nurse and placed her phone on the bed. She sat on the edge, watched the door and tapped her foot.

A sprite young nurse came running in. The nurse's crisp turquoise scrubs contrasted harshly against her red hair.

"Hi Angela," said Ms. Nikki.

"What can I do for you?" Angela asked while poring through blood work and diagnostic data from her folders, never looking up quite long enough to make Ms Nikki feel seen.

"I'm bored as all hell. Can I walk around a bit?"

"Of course. Some of the patients like to meet by the vending machines down the hall."

Ms. Nikki rolled the I.V. stand with her as she searched for the vending machines. Around a corner, sparsely occupied plastic chairs with thin cotton cushions faced a television suspended on the wall. One woman had fallen asleep slumped in her chair but kept her closed eyes fixed on the screen.

A televangelist with veneers much too large for his mouth stared soullessly out of the television. Ms. Nikki found a spot near the edge of the chairs in the middle of the pack and sat down next to a portly man in his mid-forties. He kept his I.V. in front of the chair next to him and ignored the television for the most part.

"Hey. How ya doin? I'm James."

Ms. Nikki turned to greet James and saw his Vietnam Veterans hat, thin-

ning eye brows, and wide smile.

"Nikki, nice to meet you. I'm good. How are you holding up?" she said with meekness and defeat that felt like an impression of someone else.

"I barely am. Damn near live here, at this point."

Ms. Nikki adjusted the taut threads that held her wig in place. A few strays fell onto her shoulder. She brushed them off and onto her crossed legs, making brief eye contact with James. He pretended not to notice the growing collection of chocolate brown hair collecting on her pants.

"It's crazy to think we got to use poison to heal, huh? We can't even get this stuff on our clothes," said James in a voice that may have once been kind but had been convinced by life to be anything other than 'soft.'

"Yeah, it's pretty far from fair-trade organic, isn't it?"

"That's the bitch of it. This treatment is made from tree bark."

"No, shit?"

"Shit you not. Ain't it all back-asswards?"

Ms. Nikki pulled her pump closer. The poison-pumping tube passed its way around the end of the arm of the chair.

"I just got that." She began to laugh; her voice rang with the tremors of life. "I'm definitely stealing it."

"Take it. I'll be here next week." He chuckled under his breath. "Maybe."

Through the tender silence, their laughter grew louder than the television.

"Did the nurses tell you about naming your I.V. bag?" said James returning to the conversation like a horse to water.

13

"They did. I call him Wayne Johnson."

"That's hysterical," he said with acquiescent humor but no laughter. "Can I call him 'The Pump'?"

"He prefers Wayne Johnson. He's going through a bit of a re-branding."

As Ms. Nikki and James continued to talk, another patient joined them. The presumptuous patient sat in the chair next to Ms. Nikki. She yanked the cord for Ms. Nikki's I.V., and the valve broke free and sprung open. Fluid flicked from the tube, and onto her shoes, then her shirt and wig.

James shot up and called for assistance. Three nurses swiftly moved Ms. Nikki into a private room. The fluid from her I.V. puddled on her pants. The green syrupy substance oozed over her clothes. Her nostrils filled with the scent of irradiated popcorn. The nurses closed the door behind her.

. . .

Justine hung up the phone and spun around in her chair to look at Michael. Her stethoscope swung around and slapped her pink scrubs on her shoulder.

"Ms. Nikki is still not picking up."

"She's at her appointment with Wayne Johnson today," said Michael.

"I have no idea what that means. Why do you keep saying that?"

"I'm sorry Nurse Justine, but that's what we call it."

Nurse Justine swept up the papers from her desk and went off to the supply room with a frustrated huff. With her right hand, she continued to dial Ms. Nikki. She returned with a thermometer and jammed it into Michael's mouth.

Michael laid his head down on the paper-covered pillow that rested at the top of his cot. He counted the number of holes in the tile directly above his head. He lost count and had to restart. Justine tried calling Ms. Nikki

again.

"She doesn't talk when she drives, either."

Justine waited with Michael until his temperature came down to 101. She left another voicemail on Ms. Nikki's phone.

…

A pay-as-you-go smart phone sat in a drawer beside a vegan cracked leather clutch wallet and a key ring with three keys: one for a Ford truck, another for a P.O. box, and the last for a door.

Outside the drawer was a white room devoid of decorations. Three nurses in head-to-toe white suits stood in the center of the room. One carried a bag, another carried soap, and another carried tongs. One nurse stripped Ms. Nikki down with the tongs and placed her clothes into the bag held open by another nurse.

As the clothes were removed, the third nurse cleaned Ms. Nikki from an arm's length away. The nurses chatted about how lucky she was not to get on her skin or it would have been much worse. Ms. Nikki shuddered at the thought that it could get worse than this.

Ms. Nikki's clothes were bagged and taken away.

Inside the drawer, the phone vibrated and rattled the keys.

…

Ms. Nikki struggled up the steps and into Falcon Field Charter School. She pushed the button on the intercom several times in succession and waited with her hand on the door. She shivered in her scrubs and cheap sandals from the hospital gift shop. Her thinning hair poked out from under her cap. The intercom buzzed, and Ms. Nikki used the door handle to support her weight on the way in.

"I'm so sorry. Where's Michael?"

"He's right here. His fever has gone down but I'd still get him to an urgent care or hospital right away."

"Thank you."

Ms. Nikki fumbled her keys into her hip pocket and reached out for Michael as he walked out of the nurse's office.

"Hey, buddy."

"Hey."

"I'm sorry it took me so long." Ms. Nikki began to pick at her leg through the lining of her pocket.

"It's okay."

"No, it's not buddy." Ms. Nikki straightened Michael's New 52 Superman shirt.

Ms. Nikki turned to Justine.

"I'm sorry. My phone was in the other room, and my clothes are ruined because of the chemo juice tree stuff, and I didn't have shoes, so I went to buy some, but my cash had to be thrown out, and my purse was in the car, so I walked barefoot to my car without my wig and"

"Wait here one second." Justine cut her off.

Justine walked back toward her office and turned to rummage through a drawer on her right. She returned with a black hoodie in her hand.

"Here you go. It might smell a little, but it'll get you home."

Ms. Nikki began to speak but fumbled over her words. Justine stopped her.

"We have to look out for each other."

Ms. Nikki took Michael's backpack and, with his hand in hers, walked him to the car. She drew a few deep breaths before turning over the engine and beginning their trip to the urgent care around the corner.

"How's Wayne?" said Michael.

"He's good but he broke today. That's why I'm late."

"Oh. Is he okay?" Michael looked out the window and saw a cardboard sign with black block writing flailing in the wind. A water bottle filled with dark yellow fluid rested in the gutter around the corner.

"He is. What do you think about calling him 'The Pump'?"

Michael chuckled. "That's funny."

The car pulled up to a stop light directly in front of an urgent care facility.

Ms. Nikki smiled out of the corner of her mouth. "Thank you. I'll be here all night. Maybe."

Will Trade for Friends

Michael sat at the dining room table alone. He was used to being alone. Years ago, he had been duct taped to a chair, the remote to a television taped to the arm of a plastic chair just within reach of his emaciated hands. He had learned and lived through the television with the remote as his mentor. He had no friends except for the ones he created. Michael was a skinny kid with straight, jet-black hair. He barely filled out the golf shirt he wore and his cargo pants were far too long. His legs swung back and forth, dangling from the edge of his chair and his feet kicked into the legs of the table.

He'd made up friends and named stains on the wall to get through the day while trapped in the chair. Now that he was at a foster home, he still named the chips in the table. He still talked to the missing paint on the walls. Nobody at the foster home wanted to sit with Michael and Michael was talking to his imaginary friends more and more.

He turned his focus from Jeff, the one-inch long scratch on the table, to his foster mother Ms. Nikki. Ms. Nikki was in her mid-forties. She was granted guardianship over Michael after the rights of his mother were severed the previous year, following thousands of movie nights.

She was busy packing lunches, which, in this case, meant organizing pre-made sandwiches and other easy- to- pack healthy foods, like carrots and oranges. Every day at lunch, Michael would never trade his sandwich but always exchanged the carrots. He had never seen carrots in different colors. He swore they tasted different. In between packing lunches, Ms. Nikki would hand each of her fosters boys a bowl of cereal and a small cup of juice.

"Ms. Nikki? How do you make friends?" Michael asked.

"Well baby, how did we become friends?"

"I don't know, but you're nice to me." Michael's voice was characteristically forlorn and unsure.

"Well, that's how you make friends baby. You're nice to people, and people are nice to you." Ms. Nikki's voice had the nourishing qualities of a cactus. Every so often, a flower would sprout from amongst the thorns. "But how do you get people to sit with you at lunch and stuff?"

"Well baby," she hesitated. "You have got to be the type of person people want to spend time with. You've got to be fun."

"Am I fun?"

"I think you're fun baby. You have a great sense of humor and you try very hard."

"Then why don't I have friends?"

"Oh baby, you do have friends. I'm your friend, and your brothers are your friends."

"They don't even want to sit with me."

"The other boys haven't been here long. They'll come around, baby."

"Do you have to do what people want to get them to like you?"

"Sometimes, baby, but you have to do what you want first. Do you understand what I'm saying?"

"I think so." Michael sat and watched Ms. Nikki load sodas and return the lunch supplies to the overflowing refrigerator. "Ms. Nikki, what is weed?"

Ms. Nikki's head swung from the refrigerator to gaze deep into Michael's eyes. "Why are you asking me that?" Her voice shot spiked arms out in all

directions in defense. Michael had stepped on her roots.

"Some kids at school said their brothers have some. What is it?"

"It is not for kids. Ever. Okay?" Ms. Nikki stared him dead in the eyes, waiting for his response. Michael was too scared to respond and averted his gaze back toward Jeff until she spoke again.

"Weed is something adults use to have fun. Some people think it's bad, but other people think it's good."
"Oh. Why?"

"I don't know baby," said Ms. Nikki, starting to become overwhelmed by the questions.

"How can it be good and bad?" asked Michael.

"Because people believe different things, bud."

"That doesn't make sense. Things are good or bad."

"A lot of the world is in the middle, buddy," Ms. Nikki had had enough of the questions, "Stop talking and eat your breakfast, baby." She slid a bowl of cereal on the table in front of Michael like an experienced bartender in a sitcom.

He stared at it, disgusted by the colors of the sugary treasures touching, and scowled. Michael began to form a plan for making friends in his head. The fingernail-sized paint chip Jeff, helped fill in the details, while the scratch in the table egged him on. Michael ate his cereal in order of color and size. He ate each type of marshmallow in order and then moved to the more boring and less magical pieces.

After finishing all the pieces he could stomach, Michael collected his lunch from Ms. Nikki. Shoes weren't allowed to be worn in the house, so they piled up by the front door. Michael pulled his shoes from the bottom of the pile. He hadn't always had shoes and was proud to have a clean pair even though they had started to fray along the sole and a hole had sprouted on the bottom.

He had not been taught how to tie his shoes and was still learning. In the meantime, he kept his shoes pre-tied in small knots with huge bunny ears. He was no longer able to work with the knots because they had become too tight, so he just crammed his foot into the shoes.

Ms. Nikki waited outside the door to hug each kid goodbye. Before the boys left to walk to school, Michael snuck back into the kitchen and rummaged through six drawers as fast as he could until he found his supplies. He peeked around the corners to avoid Ms. Nikki's gaze. He didn't want to be caught wearing his shoes inside. He pulled a plastic baggie from the sixth drawer and ran back to the front door. He snatched his backpack off the hook and stepped outside.

Michael and his brothers began to walk to the bus stop. Michael yelled behind them that they were leaving for school, but Ms. Nikki who was already smoking on the back porch with a Chihuahuas and a pit pull pawing at her ankles.

On the way to school, the brothers played little games with each other. They would zig-zag across the street dodging cars, and they would race between street lights. If they were early enough, they used their allowance on the elote man, whose route started next to the house and opposite the parked off-duty ice cream truck.

The shops along the way to school had not been given the homogenous grey and brown paint job that made Michael feel so uneasy in other neighborhoods. These stores still had color, and Michael liked color everywhere but in his food. Walking past the shops as they opened was like being at the fair. Echoes of faint music always rattling from behind some window.

Michael walked at the back of the pack and was never invited to play the games. Even when he would join the races, he would be ignored. Even if he won, they would pretend he'd never raced, but Michael kept count himself. He'd raced the other boys forty-seven times and had won four of them.

The boys talked about the new video game they were playing and argued

about how best to set up the boundaries for their newest game. They would race from the front of the pink house to the green salon at the end of the street using only their left legs. The boys got together in a line, and Michael decided he wanted a chance too. He jumped up to the start line at the crack in the sidewalk and kicked back his right leg.

"Ready, set, go!"

The boys started hopping along the side of the road. Michael was never the fastest, or the most athletic, but with the imposed limitation, he was much closer to the other boys. He usually had a chance to compete in these types of competitions. In a straight race, he would have been toast immediately.

He finished in second place, beating the younger of his brothers but losing to the elders. The race finished a few hundred feet from the bus stop, and the kids walked the rest of the way to meet up with their friends. Michael turned to his little brother. "Good race. You'll probably beat me next time, cause you're fast."

"You weren't even racing," said his little brother with a hostile scowl on his face.

"Why not?"

Michael's little brother didn't take the time to answer the question. The boys walked over to a group of their friends and left Michael standing alone halfway in the street. The boys sat in a circle going through their Japanese trading cards. They compared which cards they had in holographic form and how many evolutions they had. Michael had many trading cards but was never invited to share them.

He crept up to the boys in the circle and pulled out his binder of cards. Each card had its own sleeve and they were organized by color and type. He saw kids negotiating for trades that were unfair, and he decided to jump in.

"You shouldn't do that trade," said Michael to a smaller girl in a yellow shirt.

"Why not?" she asked. "I want a good water card."

"Cause your card is more rare."

"Oh. Is that cause it's shiny?"

"Yeah, I have an extra dragon I can trade you."

As the conversation continued kids from the group began to peel off and find new places to stand. They left, one by one, until Michael was standing with just the girl in the yellow dress. She delicately placed her new dragon card in the front pocket of her binder, ended the conversation and ran off to be with her friends.

The older boys isolated themselves at the edge of the bus stop huddled around their phones and watched videos of 360 no-scopes. Michael stood by himself until the bus pulled up and everybody hopped into line. Michael made his way to the back of the line by a field of weeds.

Murmurs of what the students did over the weekend punctuated Michael's anxieties. Michael backed slowly toward the fence of the abandoned field. He crossed his palms behind his back as he stepped toe-to-heel. Quick and trembling hands felt along the jagged chain-link fence. He dropped his butt, reached down, and then stuffed his fingers between the ragged links. He filled up his plastic bag and shoved it into his back pocket.

As the bus filled up, all the cool kids sat in the back and kept up their conversations. Michael sat in the front of the bus, right behind the bus driver. The bus made multiple stops. Michael knew these children even less. People filled the empty seats next to their friends, but Michael sat alone. Surrounded, toward the middle of the bus, sat the girl in yellow who was still looking at her new dragon.

At the final bus stop, a group of rowdy kids got on the bus. They stopped as they approached Michael.

"Did you bring it?" asked the largest boy under his breath. His face was covered in pock marks and the small cuts of an amateur barber.

"Yeah, I told you I could get some at the bus stop," said Michael. He was excited to have someone so cool talking to him.

"Don't talk so loud man. You'll get us all in trouble."

"Okay. Do you want it?" Michael rasped as if he were out of breath.

"Of course, we'll come grab the bag at lunch," said the short one with tight elastic clothes. Michael thought he looked remarkably like a mango. "Cool. Do you guys want to eat lunch with me?"

The boys laughed. "No, we'll grab the bag after."
"Alright."

The bus arrived at school, and Michael's first classes seemed to move by slower than usual. He went to a different part of the school than the kids from the bus stop. Those kids rotated classrooms, but he stayed in the same class all day. He did art first and then practiced spelling and history before lunch. After lunch, he had a longer recess than they did.

On his way to lunch, Michael noticed dogs smelling at the lockers in the hallways. He saw the German Shepherds before he noticed that their handlers were police officers. They wore full tactical gear and walked from locker to locker with the dogs. The school principal followed the officers with a ring of keys in his hand.

The principal was a middle-aged man with a receding hairline. The hair on the back of his head had also begun to thin, and as a result, he had a horrible sunburn. The crown of his head was beet red and had begun to peel. When the principal became nervous, he picked at the skin on his head. As he walked down the hallway with the police, he peeled away the skin and allowed the flakes to fall on the shoulders of his suit.

As Michael went to his locker to collect his lunchbox, the principal reached out and grabbed onto Michael's arm. His grip startled Michael and the force caused his knees to buckle. He fell butt first toward the ground. The principal yanked him back to his feet.

"Why don't you wait for me by my office?" said Principal Skinner.
"What about lunch?" said Michael.

"You can eat outside my office." said Principal Skinner tugged Michael
down the hall. He pulled Michael through the halls faster than he could
walk, so his feet began to drag.

"Sit down and wait."

"Okay."

Michael sat in the chair outside the principal's office for what seemed like
forever. He invented names for the drawings and smudges on the wall.
Over time, they got individual back-stories. Some smudges were adven-
tures or pirates, and others were spies or soldiers. Eventually, Michael
heard small beeps coming from police radios in the hall.

Principal Skinner burst in and opened the door to his office. The police
followed him in. One was tattooed and muscular. He looked like one of
the soldiers from Michael's table. The other officer was just as muscular
but much taller. His eyes widened, and he smiled at Michael briefly as he
entered.

"Come on in, Michael."

Michael walked into the principal's office. The room smelled like syr-
up and chicken skin. The smell wouldn't have been bad if the chicken
containers had been removed from the office. Michael sat in a rolling
scratchy chair that gave off a concentrated version of the stench. Two
police officers blocked the entrance to the principal's office.

"Did you bring something to school today, Michael?" said Principal Skin-
ner with an edge of inflated authority, emboldened by armed assistance.
"I brought my trading cards and my lunch."

"That's not what I mean. Did you bring anything bad to school today?"

"No. I don't think so."

"Anything that's not allowed at school?

"No--" Michael stopped hard after he spoke. The thought of his plastic bag popped into his head.

"One of the kids at school told us you might have a bag of marijuana."

"What's that?" Michael asked with the heavy up-speak of genuine confusion.

"Pot or weed. Drugs. Do you have any?"

The police officers crept forward.

"Oh, yeah. I guess. Am I in trouble?"
"Probably, kid. Just give us the weed."

"Okay."

Michael reached into his backpack and pulled out a plastic sandwich bag of weeds. Small thorns poked out from the corners of the bag. A large beetle was trapped inside crawling on the zipper. Michael's eyes started to well up with tears. He wasn't good at being in trouble. As Michael placed the bag onto the principal's desk, the police officers came into the office and huddled over him.

"Here. Please don't tell Ms. Nikki."

"She's already on her way."

The principal and officers examined the bag and turned it over in their hands. The bag didn't contain marijuana or any other type of illegal drug; the bag was packed to the brim with common garden weeds. The tall slender officer chortled.

"What is this, Michael?" asked the principal as the officers tore through Michael's backpack.

"That's weed. Isn't it, Mr. Skinner?"

Principal Skinner let out a sigh and hung his head. Hunched and defeated, he waddled over to the officers and led them outside.

Michael couldn't hear much, but he caught small strings of words. "On the Spectrum…Suspension…Autistic…Sorry."

The officers left the office, and Principal Skinner sat with his butt on the desktop in front of Michael. The fat from his rear spilled over the top of his shirt and the edges of the table.

"You're going to be given three days of in-school suspension for bringing weed to school."

"Why?'

"Because marijuana isn't allowed on campus. It is illegal."

"That's not fair," Michael said half-heartedly. He knew he should be in trouble, but this was how people on the television acted when they were in big trouble.

"Oh, it's very fair. You're getting off easy."

"Whatever," he said flippantly. He had gotten that quip from sit-coms with teenagers. Ms. Nikki said that if he wanted to be treated like a teenager, then he had to act like one. He took that to heart.

"Ms. Nikki is on her way here to take you home. I'm disappointed in you."

It took a while for Ms. Nikki to arrive at the school. Michael was walked out to Ms. Nikki's truck, after the principal informed Ms. Nikki of what had happened. As soon as the principal walked away from the car, Ms. Nikki lit up a cigarette and turned to Michael.

"You know what you did was wrong, right?" Ms. Nikki was being careful to hold the cigarette outside the window. She craned her head into the wind to take a drag and exhale.

"Yeah, I just wanted to have friends," said Michael.

"That's not how you make friends, baby."

Michael didn't want to talk about that. He wanted to talk about a new word. "What's Autism?" he asked.

Ms. Nikki choked on her cigarette smoke.

"Where did you hear that, baby?"

"The police officer and the principal said it."

"Oh, well…" Ms. Nikki tried to steady herself, "It means a brain works different than other people's brains. They're the same. Just wired different."
"Am I autism?"

"Yeah, buddy. You are, but it doesn't make you any different."

"Is that why I don't have friends?"

"You don't have friends because kids are too busy learning how to be themselves to learn how to be your friend." Ms. Nikki took one last long and luxurious pull from her cigarette and put it out in the cup holder.
"That doesn't seem right."

"It's not, baby. Just give them time. They'll come around. I promise."

The school bell rang, and class was released for the day. Michael and Ms. Nikki sat in the school parking lot and waited for the rest of the brothers. As they waited, the girl in the yellow dress came up to the truck. She walked over to the window and peeked in on her tippy-toes.

"You're the kid that traded me earlier."

"Yeah. I'm Michael."

"I'm Vanessa. See you tomorrow, Michael."

"I won't be in class tomorrow. But maybe I'll see you later."

"Okay."

The little girl ran off as Michael's brothers piled into the truck. They were all talking about what Michael had done. They talked about the dogs and the police officers as if it were an episode of television in which Michael had emerged the hero. For the first time, Michael felt seen.

"Looks like Vanessa might be your friend," said Ms. Nikki.

"Yeah," said Michael gleefully, "and I didn't get in trouble for the water dragon."

Acknowledgement

"It is hard to believe that a man is telling the truth when you know that you would lie if you were in his place." – Henry Louis Mencken

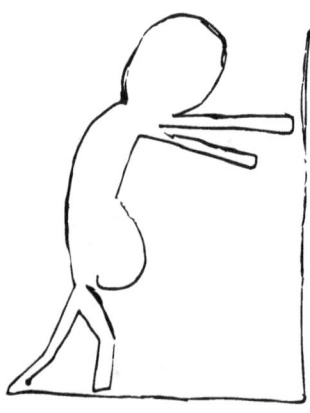

Marcus Sterling Campbell is a poet and film enthusiast from Phoenix, Arizona. He enjoys long walks down dark alleys and sitting in his cave doing as much nothing as possible. You can find him trolling for used books and movies or yelling at a screen about nonsense. His work can be found scattered across the web or @marcus_s_campbell on social media.

For best experience, please rotate book 180° before continuing.

33